In Stories We Thunder

Sundress Publications • Knoxville, TN

Editor: Tierney Bailey
Editorial Assistants: Kanika Lawton
Managing Editor: Tennison Black
Editorial Interns: Finnegan Angelos, Anna Mirzayan, Brooke Shannon, and
Hailey Small

Colophon: This book is set in Averia Serif Libre
Cover Image: "En El Bosque," by Jennifer (Yen) Ospina
Cover Design: Kristen Ton
Book Design: Tennison Black

In Stories We Thunder
V. Ruiz

Acknowledgments

The author extends their gratitude to the following journals for publishing earlier versions of these poems:

Action California Planned Parenthood, "War Paint"
Black Warrior Review, "The Genesis"
Calyx, "In a fever I write to you"
Carve, "Life Advice from a Girasol" (nominated for a Pushcart)
Dryland Lit., "An Ode to Nopales"
The Florida Review, "Las Mujeres Caídas"
Fugue, "Lineage of Eggs" (finalist in the 2019 Poetry Prize)
Hayden's Ferry Review, "We Learn to Hold the Sky" (nominated for a Pushcart)
LunaLuna, "Remedy for vulnerability"
Madwoman Etc Zine, "Why I Show You These Brujerías" and "A Sonnet of Pasos"
New South Journal, "Muñeca"
Permafrost Magazine, "Puta Found" (nominated for a Pushcart)
Read Water, "La Caída"
Star 82 Review, "Poison Lines"
Tinderbox Poetry, "Sangre" and "Hair of the Dog"
Wizards in Space, "Relief"

Table of Contents

Before Birth

The quilt of expansive sky weighs—
Teeth clamp on skin—
Man, can God bite hard.
But these hands push through soil,
Rise from the grave.
A nebula explodes in us.
And we burst into new galaxies.
Exist in the silver thread of the night.

If I told you the whole story it would never end...
What's happened to me has happened to a thousand women.
—Doña Rosita la Soltera, Federico García Lorca

I.

The Genesis

I once loved a man who planted obsidian
between my ribs in sueños.
He called the stone a gift, an anchor to keep my cuerpo
from drifting into the sea of premonitions.

The stone keeps me from reaching the cielo,
and even with sunflower eyes I only find La Luna.

I dream of my hija before she is born.

~~I tried to chip his memory from my chest.~~
~~I tried to melt his stone into ink.~~
His weight remains buried in my bones.
I translate this darkness into omens.

The women in my familia speak the language of dreams:
The whites of our eyes cut from moonstone.
Lullabies sung in tears. Stories of how we survive.

After the obsidian man I was weighed down—
Men with fists and their breath.
I know nothing of strength other than
the hand's ability to cradle a candle through storms.

I swallow the syllable seeds of her name,
mold azucar morena into something too vulnerable
a sweet so easily crumbled.

~~I tried to warn her of the black in my chest.~~
~~I tried to bury his stone behind my corazón.~~
I gifted my daughter a ruby glint of my spirit and sometimes
I fail to remember she is a chispa floating from my flame.

Beneath the light of a thousand tiny suns
I point out the constellations of the women who have survived.
I swallow the syllable seeds of these myths.

Aesop Remix for my Hija: The Ant and the Dove

The paloma loved the taste of tiny things,
of crawling things, of delicacies granted without struggle.

The ant saw only white wings stretching wide,
saw the beak and understood itself to be a thing
that could be swallowed in a blink.

Hija, maybe the paloma thought about eating the ant.
Maybe it believed it would be so easy
to swallow it whole.

But it chose not to,
as in: there is always a choice.

Even if it had been a paloma born mala—one who pondered,
who bent forward to smell the ant—
there was always going to be a moment
where the paloma either decided to swallow the ant or spare it.

Lineage of Eggs

✧

The first time my mother got her period she didn't know what was happening.
Spent eggs spilled out of her in rust,
I thought I was dying.
My abuela handed her diaper thick cloth
said *this is the price you pay to be a woman.*

✧

My mother didn't know she was having sex
when she got pregnant.
I didn't look—didn't like—didn't know—
what was happening. Didn't know her cuerpo
was so ready to hold someone else's yolk.

✧

Years later she's married to a man who cracks
her spine, spills blood to her skin, her egg white eyes
turning black, cracks her costillas in half
like a wishbone after she cut her ovaries
to stop any more eggs from being robbed by knuckles.
He whispers over her chips, wishes she would be an empty shell—
only of use to fertilize.

✧

At seventeen I find a man with a family
obsessed with eggshell skin.
He parades me around on a spoon—on good days—
until I gain weight, until he's drunk, until I tumble to concrete
my skin spilling bloodied yolk.

✧

I start giving myself limpias at eighteen.
Wipe my skin with an egg
think of all the potential held in a fragile shell.
My abuela calls it *brujerías*, calls it *esas cosas malas*.
But I feel the way egg holds life inside,
feel the meal brewing below my stomach,
feel the quiver of something sparking and spreading inside.

✧

Nine years later I see my egg with limbs spreading out of a shell.
See her tumble stumble never crack, think of all the ways
the world could break her, think of her body and the unborn inside.
My hija is allergic to eggs.
She doesn't understand yet why I slide them along my skin
or why I lean in before splitting and spilling them on a sartén
why I pray to the sizzle and say *I see all that you could be.*

Sleep Requires Breath and a Body That Forgets

Black static bleeds
along my eyes as I bleed
on the seats
and wonder if I'll give myself away.

✧

I said
          No
He said
          Let's go
Wait—I said, I think I said,
          I'm not ready for this

We were kissing.
Then a car—No, a van.
I remember saying, *I want to be alone.*
With him, he said.
                    Too much whiskey breath. Need
air.   Need
stars, and breath, and a room with no walls.
He said his car had AC.   Air Cold Cold Air Fresh Air
I said yes.
Did I ask to leave?
          "You said you wanted to be alone."
Asthma. Hourglass sand throat. Glass on lips.

I, I don't think I'm ready for this.
        "You're already here."
His weight. His arms crush—
No, his hand
smothers.

   ✧

      THE BODY
FLOATS
FINGERS TRACE SHAPES
IN CLOUDS
A POPCORN CEILING

Can't breathe. Did I
say yes? His tongue
drowns. Can't
remember.
He said
"You should probably clean yourself up
        you bled everywhere."

I Don't Think Blood Knows How to Forget a Bruise

Memories are ghosts:
beings that come alive in fragments.
Sometimes when I laugh
I hear his chuckle.
Sometimes when my lover slaps my ass

I feel the pat of a man's hand
on a mattress saying *come,*
lie here with me,
do not be afraid.

I have been consumed
by beasts—men so willing
to make a soft body turn rough.
I am not afraid of what lies in darkness.

I am afraid of the voices
I must carry through the world
the sounds of the wounded and all
the ones so willing to wound.

The Fables We Keep From Our Children

Somewhere there is a cocoon being prodded—
the mariposa's wings forced to unfurl
before being taught about winds that push—bend—break.

In a park beneath a tree lie discarded candy wrappers
and scattered beads from a torn best-friend bracelet.

Near the sea is a sand castle shaped by chubby clay hands
overpowered by a riptide swollen from murky waters.
Everyone is taught how to swim in still waters
without learning the ocean can turn too quick.

Beneath a wooden pier, a family of oysters cling
to the only home they know, unable to predict
when sea hunters will pry apart their shell
trying to find a pearl to claim as their own.

When did we all become little red
on an island inhabited by wolves?

Muñeca

Muñeca lived in a dollhouse with brick colored walls thin enough to be pierced by bullets or a fist. Hands moved her from corner to chair to bed but Muñeca never complained. At least she had the night. Nights where she laid with a stitched mouth on sticker tiles watching La Luna dance across her window, waiting for the luz to blind her glass eyes.

She had pillow flesh that gave way to any finger's touch. Her body did not need a spine because a spine could be crushed and she found it was easier to heel if she learned to cave beneath weight.

There were boys who would steal her from the dollhouse, place her next to soldiers saying she's the esposa and her husband is at war and the hole they carved was home. And the boys would *bang boom shoot* green men against each other splashing her with dirt that never reached her eyes.

Her cheeks were Mother's lipstick smudged into drawn circles. Mother always said *queda te joven* because youth was a gift that bought her time. Hairy hands rarely craved something so doll-like. But the cheeks like rosas didn't always work.

Sometimes calloused hands would come and cinch her waist with a ribbon, puff balls of algodón beneath her dress, walk her around saying *misses, I like your vestido, misses come with me to dinner tonight, misses you seem so much older than you are.* And even then Muñeca tried to embrace the dress up game.

Muñeca's hair was made of thick yarn black as the nights she was flipped upside down. The yarn was a pillow for her tired head. She tried to remember it was easier being soft. The open wall of her dollhouse reminded her of this. It was always easier being soft beneath sour breath and smoky hands.

But one day Mother came and lifted her away. And Mother's eyes were not glass because glass didn't make oceans of tears. Her soft hands lifted her and carried her outside beneath the Sol and placed her on burning plastic black where she smelled rotten potato and diaper air.

Here she waited. But she saw stars. Saw full moon light that didn't blind her but made the smells easier to bear than the Sol's boiling heat.

Then one morning a man came. Wearing night sky clothing and the man said *My what a beautiful doll*. And she was afraid of his calloused hands. But the man had gentle fingers and he said *I cannot throw you out. Not with eyes like a moonless night*. And the man bent down and carved a hole like the one the boys called home. He said *Do not be afraid*. And he placed her inside and covered the hole with handfuls of dirt and Muñeca remembered, finally, what it was like to sleep.

Ars Poetica

I slice crescent lunas from my fingertips and bury them
in your eyes. You ask me how it feels to be made
of night. Sometimes in the bruja's hour I hear my sangre
howl. I tell you that on nights when the Luna is tucked away
I forget my own name. I become the cursive of my teeth:
all gnashing and grinding. I become obsidian with all
it's reflecting and projecting. Soy creatura.
Un animal. I run from your day
bury myself in the depth of script, give myself
to the translation of tongues. With this body
I ask the mundo to display itself.
I pull the tides. I show you what it means
to break on land. When the Luna becomes opal—
a pupil to this universe—I harvest the nails in your eyes
try to show you the meaning in all I buried.

From These Wounds

Sycamore trees peel bark as they form new flesh.
Their sickly appearance predating nothing
more than the creation of new skin.

I have scars doctors say could have been avoided—
places where my blade dug too deep
fatty tissue poked from underneath.

How many other beings use scars
as a foundation for new life?

My wounds are afraid
of addressing the hand with the weapon
dancing across my skin.
Like the trees, I just shed
never believing in what follows.

And I think we're all like that.
We are gaping.

II.

Aesop Remix for My Hija: A Raven and a Swan

Don't look to the lake to find other ravens.
They're all in the sky
all letting their night side slice
the clouds. Listen Hija,
the swans are all angry and bitter anyways.
Don't eat the weeds they thrive on.
Don't dip into the waters imagining
yourself blended in a sea of white—
it won't work.
And trying to lighten away the darkness
only leads to feathers that feel sickly and not your own.
You'll try to pluck them
before you accept they will not change.
Yes, Hija, you may live in a land with a wide reach
and a lake where swans consider themselves queens,
but I'll tell you this:
there are so many more bodies
of land with birds like you.
There are oceans with pelicans
who could eat up a swan.
There are forests dripping with rainbowed macaws
who can understand all songs
without cutting out their tongues.
The land you're tossed in with wings dripping or clipped
is not always the land you will belong to,

is not always the land
where you will find yourself
in the praised reflections.

On Learning to Hate Diner Milkshakes

At 15 our biggest worry was finding a ride and hiding extra clothes to smoke in: stubby half cigarettes we put out hours ago and tucked away in baggies. We never wasted a puff and always smoked to the filter. Sometimes we panicked over finding purses big enough to carry extra sweaters—the perfect zip-up that hugged, that could be unzipped to show just enough cleavage to get an invite to some battle of the bands, though there seemed to be a different battle of the bands every week.

K never had to worry about calculating the perfect position of a zipper. She was near-flat chested, which made her strappy shirts fit my chest like I was sketched in bold marker. And I'd lend her my socks and a bra even though her mother had already taken her out to shop for pushups. And K would tighten her belt so that little lumps of skin folded over the side, so she could have "love handles" just like mine—which at that point I was trying to vomit away.

I've forgotten the taste of bottomless french fries in the diner where we cashed out dollars for nickels—where we sang along to the jukebox like it belonged to us. Sometimes I still see K from before, fifteen and reflected in the steel of a milkshake glass, the K from those times where we called ourselves opposites like it bonded us.

Before her mother began labeling me as trouble, or the cause of K falling into the swirl of a glass pipe—though she was gone long before she tasted those billowy clouds. The last time we spoke was on the phone. I was off bleeding at my own hands and she was somewhere in an alley taking artsy shots and claiming to be the next Twiggy.

Why I Show You These Brujerías

1.

Once, I loved a boy
who begged me to conjure us
an escape. I spooned

dirt en mis manos, spit in soil
and molded a four-door as I sang

for La Luna. By the night of the next
black sky he rode off in a paid-for Corolla

and I sat alone with the ghost of the moon
picking dirt from under my fingernails.

My Dios, how many times have we
willingly given our power away?

2.

It started with the click-clank of apothecary bottles
Filled with yerba buena and manzanilla.

It started with a collection of Goddamn
word fuckery in spells like prayers. It started

with tracing of veins in sage—always
asking for permission before plucking.

Now we carry on: drum on hides beneath
the splattered night. When the pounding

becomes an echo we find our voices
in the sounds that return as ghosts.

3.

Once I claimed love spells naive, forgot
the way I whispered fantasies

in ears while chasing sigils on bare chests.
Looked away from the way my fingers drove

me to pleasure with the image of what would
eventually come to be. Maybe brujes who

light inscribed blood candles are more skilled
in taming the fuego I wish I knew nothing about.

4.

Does anyone ever tire

of the attention given to

the filigree embroidered

on Mystery's cloak?

5.

I am pounding herbs in a bowl
     made of volcanic stone.
        I leave

the mixture in a glass jar—
     let the Sol have it—
        charge it.

This is how the tierra teaches
     us to heal our hurts
        how it gives

the power to make for ourselves
     a new fate.

6.

It started as magic: an innocent idea
of spells as pastel thoughts. Color as healing.

Now we claim brujerías. Claim a release
from the world's hands on our flesh.
We take what exists
and cradle it

in a new direction: Now
we are a candle lit
at the center of a monsoon.

Sprouting

In the weathered wood
of a fence in Ocean Beach
newborn greenery grows.

And it could be a fucking tree
for all I know, or maybe
a fickle rose,
but it spreads—riots
without questioning its blueprint.

Yet here I am unable to sit still,
questioning what I am becoming,
where I am growing.

In the crack of the madera
two leaves plume out to breathe
salted air—
crash to the dance of waves.

Remedy for Vulnerability

Amor/ the first time i orgasmed/ with you my stained glass eyes shattered/
beneath your Sol-bright gaze/ breaking me into a puddle/ of mosaic geometrics
unable to be puzzle-pieced/ back into the mural i resiliently crafted/ i spilled
honey/ luring the residents of the anthill beyond the swell of your home/
begging the Mother Queen with her millions of eggs/ to gift me her unborn/
swallowing their potential/ anendorfic treatment to remove this love sickness/
this oxytocin bond/ sometimes too much/

Statistics

My mind is a six-lane highway divided by a crumbling median
mess, cracked glitz reflectors, cycas palms split by tires,

and way too many dented guard rails. What I'm really saying
is that I am a history of accidents.

I am a history of imperfect timing resulting in 1 in 5000 car deaths
happening *only* here. A sugar skull cabeza marked by crosses,

and flowers, and names of all the people who were in the wrong
intersections of me. See, my body is a freak occurrence

of too many hot winds colliding at once. And I think the space between
my legs must hold the bermuda triangle because

I've only ever seen the people who love between them
lose their breath, fall into an endless blue

before they disappear and are nothing
but the memory I lay to rest in a blackbox.

While Tracing Shapes in the Sky, I Teach My Hija About the World

1.
Orion's belt is easily identified
by the equidistant holes in
his stomach. Stars form a man:
primal—a hunter with a legacy.

But Hija, all I see is an arrow aimed
at seven Pleiades sisters forever running
from his lust.

2.
Sometimes I search the night sky
for the estrella's effervescence just to watch
the flicker of the dying flames too far to give warmth.

Planets are rarer but steady existence
does nothing to intrigue those seeking
a flashing distraction.

3.
I once met a man of the moon,
moon child Cancer was he.
He moved waters with forces unseen
just to prove he was more La Luna than me.

Contrasting my Capricorn nature
Crab boy told me, "We're mostly water
and if you can move rivers
you can play with minds."

But silly moon child knew nothing
of power unclaimed.
We may be mostly H2o
but our soul is fire to gasoline.
I'm the moon's daughter, and he,

just another boy banging rocks
to make sparks.

4.
Someone once said galaxies
can pass through one another unfazed—
the distance between stars too great
to touch, too wide to collide

into black holes.
When our bodies crashed
I never felt you.
Maybe we're too grand to connect.

Maybe the space between
is how we touch.

5.
Mars makes me think of the Tower tarot.
The red planet glows: A coal
waiting to burn out in bonfire pools.

I hear the Rover on Mars sings "Happy Birthday"
to itself each year.
Music springing to life in once dead air
from something so inorganic.

6.
Imagine an ant seeing our pupils
as planets greater than their existence.
Knowing without care makes us human
but harnessing the cosmos made us
believe ourselves Gods.

In a Fever I Write to You

And say all birds remind me of you,
and the time we went to an exotic bird store.
We each held a macaw and you leaned in and whispered
to the white one with a crown on my shoulder.
And it's pupils widened and shut into a needle
just before it leaned in to snatch up
my turquoise necklace. You told me as you pried out
the stone from its beak that you and I once lived as birds
on an island so far from here.

I still feel the berries in my belly roll around
with early morning worms.
And my hands are still talons
trying to pick up any weak thing to take it to the skies
so it can feel all that blue before it's consumed.

My letters to you always start with *I miss you.*
before I delete the words and change it to
I will never forgive you and I think I'm still
trying to understand how I can exist in both of these spaces,
how a bird can be winged but flightless.

Life Advice from a Girasol

Let's become these eyes, only

        these eyes. Plant these semillas

    in the gravity of soil.

      We don't know how to love

    without   exposing.   We spooned

silence into our bellies until the silk cradled what

      we didn't know needed to be held.

           We've unearthed

our roots so many times just to ground ourselves in new homes.

Let's become the rising

        ((When the Earth of this body
            is all craters
       where does all the spent dirt go?))

    sprout: the arms, the hands, the fingers.

We are not afraid to claw

our way through shadows.

Let's become the stem that bends for a peep

at the nude Sol: not caring which way the clouds

string out, finding our ecliptic path without the blinding.

We are all but spinning girasols, turning,

watching the same oscuridad distort before
our seed-eyes.

Let's become the brown before the cascade of yellow—We are more than this

becoming   more than this blooming.

III.

Aesop Remix for my Hija: The Cock and the Fox

Maybe the fox had a familia to feed.
Maybe the fox couldn't eat
the berries cuz they were nightshades,
or the fruit of that one tree
caused some type of allergic reaction.
Maybe the fucking
apples were too out of reach and hard
for the fox's teeth. So many vegan animals frowning
upon the fox stealing away chicks.
Where was the scolding when the fox ate up all those gusanos
the ones eating away at the roots?
And that cock was so boastful:
waking the farmer and the farmyard to tell everyone
he had caught a thief. Why are foxes always thieves?
They're making do with what they have.
Why don't people blame the pinche farmer
who planted a home right between the strip of land
the fox used to hunt conejos in.
Hija, I want you to understand that a thief who's been stolen from is only
fighting to get back what is theirs.
Hija, the cage doesn't mean the caught is a monster,
and malo isn't so clear when laws are written

by those who had the privilege
of forcing out anyone who stood in the way.

Poison Lines

My abuela lines the walls
of our house with poison chalk
when she knows the rains are coming.
A makeshift border to guard against
the ants who smell the threat
of falling water. As they brace
for the wet to soak their backs
do they fear the white
lines blocking their hope
of reaching dry land?

Jailbird Burritos

My Tío loved to cook jail food.
A sketchy twist of top chef.
He created countless dishes of top ramen
and hot cheetos mixed with snuck-in packets of mayo.

My Tío hated my (step) father. One time
he showed me how to spit in his margarita.
How to pull up phlegm of words unsaid
and fling it in the glass. And my (step) father,
smug motherfucker, would sit there licking his lips.

And my Tío and I would laugh
as we downed chilled forties in the park.
Mocking and drinking was never enough.
After alcohol's release, he craved rock candy,

craved billows of clouds. My uncle
could make stew out of scraps, and wine
out of bruised fruit. But when he died
all I tasted was menthol and meth.

After Solstice

There are children in cages cutting wings into their arms throwing pretend aluminum furniture at faces blocked by chain-link fences. And I'm watching this unfold from my phone—some privileged-ass shit—watching pharmaceutical dope being pumped in their arms until children drugged with the silver diamonds of the mountains of Guatemala of Children robbed What does a child hold when they're stolen from the breast of their mother? they're not but birds flying wishing the fence to be the Chihuahua of Honduras. of sunlight and their color made to become untouched white marble, a greyscale image to look back on years later. Do not tell me you cannot hear the wails for their áma for their papa. Think of the youngest think of the toddlers in diapers and how they can barely walk straight, but see them stand trial.

Smoke Clouds

You said you discovered meth in the cells.
The world insides got no time, it's all just colder
and darker. Everything we use to escape
out here is much more needed when
the only company you have is scratches in the gray

counting down a release. When you count days by
the black that consumes you and the wails in the night.
Out here the city didn't trust you and what you'd seen.

The days you were released were always celebrations
for everyone but you. Everyone who thought it a start over
and you couldn't help but ask *when did the other life end?*
Everyone wanted to know where you would make a living

where you would spend your time and how many AA classes
you were willing to attend. They wanted to know what you
would do to change. No one asked you how they could help.
No one asked you what the world felt like after living in all those walls.

Once you told me *The sky is brighter, the sun's hot as hell, and each*
of these fucking white bulbs is just a reminder. Your hija is an adult now
like me wandering around the world
wondering what it means to have a felon for a father,
wondering why theft and drugs can mark a man for life.

Puta Found

Bitch.
The word is used
as Fuck in English.

Prostituta. Hija de una puta. All daughters will be putas
In someone's eyes.

    "Puta may refer to:
    Puta (deity) a minor Roman goddess of pruning[1]."

"It's a very transcendent[2] word" star Pedro Pascal (of *Narcos*) said.

    Is calling someone a puta empowering or offensive?
Comment below!"
        #teamputa

    Puta Madre describes their restaurant as a tribute[3]
    to the Mexican Brothel Mother from 1918.

The Hippy Seed Company Offers: The Puta Madre Pepper
Brought to you by your Chili Seed Experts.

---

[1] Reduce the extent of (something) by removing superfluous or unwanted parts.

[2] Surpassing the ordinary; exceptional.

[3] An act statement, or gift intending to show gratitude, respect, or admiration.

Every single plant is nursed (*are these white putas breastfeeding their plants now?*) by us.

Some white dude: "Puta must mean ally in Spanish because Mexican dudes keep calling me that"

Sangre

Loca loca loca
The word is dissonance:
Cheekbone meeting palm
The static of a mic
Turned on too soon

It started
//with a safety pin\\
Started with gentle
//metal beneath skin\\
Craving safety of thought
//in the glide, the glide, the glide\\

A pin only pierced the memories
Without letting them bleed
Mamá counts the scars on my hand
But fails to see the rubies peeking through jeans

It is only years later that I learn
The Tarahumara of Chihuahua healed
Through bleedings—rivers of red
From a curandera's precision

The knowledge unblocked
A dam of guilt

Loca loca loca
When all I wanted was to find Dios
En mi sangre

War Paint

Clubs blast scratched punk.
We shrug on torn fishnets. After all,
a tear is fashion and sometimes
holes say more about who we are
than all the fabric that remains.
My hermanas don hoops and flannel,
paint labios red to prepare
for polaroids and sweaty brick
wall fucking, or maybe because
we know any snapshot could be
on a poster across town, or
a mugshot in a file, or a form of
evidence post-mortem.

The Little Deer
  —*after Frida Kahlo*

The background is forest with dead trees and broken branches. Far away is the stormy, lightning-lit sky which brings some hope, but the deer will never be able to reach it.

I tried to be spiritual once and discovered
I fail at transcendence. I don't want it.
I find the curve of my teeth in the stars

my own nails in the crescent moon
my wails in the roar of the sea.
Even in my pulse
I only hear my own fantasmas.

In the deer's eyes I find my reflection.
Wound me with your arrows, Dios.
This body is nothing
beyond my own mouth my own words
what these manos choose to make in this life

IV.

Aesop Remix for my Hija: Two Cocks and an Eagle

There will be people you cannot stand,
but two beaks in battle mean sangre will be shed—
what I mean, Hija, is choose your fights wisely.
Don't be afraid to draw blood,
or shed it, in effort of pecking out ojos
that cannot bear your feathers
that prove home is another farmland far off.
Peck at the wings of those who think their span
somehow enables them to flap out
smaller birds or wingless beings.
Most importantly: If you are pecked,
and your wings are clipped by another
being's mouth, step into the shadows. Rest.
Let your wounds become scarred flesh.
Sometimes in your healing you'll find
the prideful forget they are also prey.

What Clarity Can Be Found in Rage Hitting Ground

The girl bows to the flame
then swallows it whole.

Tell the sky gods they've never
seen a girl grow worlds

out of a burning like this, never seen a girl
ignite light with only a forked tongue.

Fire breathers are all about purging the molten.
Spitting out what is too hot to bear.

This girl wants nothing more than to be
the flames: the girl will be a lit Santa Muerte vela

she says *watch as I make life out of this chaos.*
Have you ever seen crystal made by the heat of lightning?

Hair of the Dog

When I dream of my grandfather
I see myself cutting off bits of his hair
As he lays in an antibiotic room
Surrounded by the beep-beep of him

I take the clippings
And grind them in my molcajete
Mix in pocketed soil dug
From the graves of plum-bruised women
Use the pestle to pulverize
The concoction with spit

—He cries clutching his hollow chest—

I take his tarred pomegranate heart
And pound it in the round of the bowl

As he begs for forgiveness I smile
Take the molcajete to my mouth and
Lick the remedio

My full mouth cannot forgive
Instead I
Take what bit my family
Cure our blood of his rabidness

The Men You Will Meet as the Star in a Play Tentatively Titled *Being Chingona in Academia*

[The Italian Man Who Fancies Himself as Non-White]
There's a 95.2% chance he will call you mamacita and a 100% chance he will say mami during sex, but it'll sound more like mommy. But, like, it's okay because he knows a little Italian.

[The Diverse Professor]
Will pat himself on the back for not being afraid to say the words Black and Brown, but will still butcher your name. He will ask you to work with ESL students, you know, cuz you're diction is so great. When he says "You speak English so well?!" Feel free to roll up his "diverse" reader and pat him on the snout while saying I'M. BILINGUAL. PENDEJO.

[The I Just Want to Help You With Your Career]
He will talk about getting you to "the top". He'll read the lines of your legs instead of the words on your resume. You'll earn patience points if he says *Let me help you gain experience, one on one* and you manage to avoid throwing the gold plated stapler at his head. Mira, if you didn't realize by now, experience is code for sex.

[The Man With the Exotic Fetish]
He will say he's not racist because he's been inside every country (He'll likely wink when he says it). He will ask you to recommend authentic Latin food and say he *just loves exotic women* while you pronounce Guacamole like your name should be Becky.

[The *I Know I'm White* Man]
He will say things like *I once dated a Latina* and the anecdotes that follow will have to do with her fire and not at all related to the conversation. When he reads your writing he will say *Now I know I'm just a white guy* as a preface to every comment. A nice hispanic girl will say, *I value your opinion.* You will probably say *hold up, you're white? Since when?*

[Fake Woke White Boy]
He will reel you in by being 100% up to date on politics without considering the weight it takes for you to be reminded of it all. He'll bring up the need for diversity in academia while mentioning the benefits it brings in making him "worldly." He'll say keep on throwing *ese español in your poetry even if no one understands* because he knows how few of us there are in this space. Consider posting his photo on Craigslist as an ad entitled: Unpaid Internship in Emotional Labor.

[White Guilt Evader]
He will apologize for the state of the world. He will post pictures of his trip to Haiti on Facebook with plenty of black children behind him. He'll brag about how the trip totally changed his life. He'll mention his views on the wall, the mistreatment of people of color in America, and make fun of the president but stay completely silent when his friends ask "But where are you really from?" This is a good chance to teach him the power of la chancla.

Her Flesh Was a Canvas he Stole

Until his final days she caved
beneath his digit mountains and
bruising spots of all he conquered.

For years she craved the static
of white noise, the drowning
of a finished beating over the screams
that weaved in the air
before the golpes began

forever knowing his palabras would cut
her soil, leaving weeds to grow years later.

We're always taught to see the warnings
never what to do with the aftermath.

Until his final days she learned
to accept the reality in the bitter
pills cracking off her teeth.

My abuela cannot | My mother cannot | I cannot
kill to survive.

Until his final days, he craved our deaths.
Nevertheless, we have made wings of our throats.

We have made a home of flight
He will not rob us of this world. We will build houses
in all this mud. We will make homes
in the swamps. We will learn
to find new worlds in the words
we pass on—in the women we become.

Lagrimas of the Guitar

Bachata brings to the tongue a taste of waterfalls on cheeks.
A style of musica that makes the guitar sing anthems for the broken.

As my body gives way to the waters, I'm reminded of a man intoxicated
By his own hips swaying. My (step) father—a man with the ability to freeze

An ocean. I never danced with him. Like oil and water I understood
That he held more weight in our lives than I. So instead I watched.

Tracked the way he pulled my mother across the room—this time
A performance this time not a dragging across carpet burning her skin.

She: a sail to navigate his life. Without music he was the storm,
The falling rain and hail—drowning us with his force.

Because we failed to recognize then
The way our bodies, like the moon, could sway tides.

Waves can still break beneath ice.

Anglerfish

I've never been one to lean to a conch shell
and hear anything more than my own heartbeat.
When I walk the ocean I never go further than knee height—
I know all the darkness will consume me.
I think night is the closest thing
we land walkers have to living in the sea
all that endless black lit by dots in the sky.
Maybe all those stars are just wounds.

Some days I drape sheets over the windows
lay beneath the weight of all the blankets I can find.
I do not know how to swim out of the pressure of these waves
these unforgiving and crashing memories.
So I lay in it. Let the suffocation pass.
I become a deep sea creature who knows how to thrive
in all this mystery. Isn't it easier to dream
in darkness? When you know the only light is your fire,
the beam of your own lighthouse.

When My First Gray Hair Arrived

I plucked it away only to watch two birth
From where the first bloomed

The fibra plumed icy cool I watched silver vines
Sprout over and over as a single hair became feather

Each time I plucked new plumage emerged thickening
Into a crown of hollow silk bones

My head becoming bird my skin giving way
To layers and ruffles I am a woman fading

To night with a boca crowning into a beak
My screams sounding more like squawks

I'm biting my own lengua to stop all this parroting
Even vocal birds can be forced to say I love you

I have a frail tongue a small mouth but I will the commands
Into my own hechizos tell myself te amo te amo te amo

In all of this fading say I will stain my insides
Regardless of this molting say

When I turn all gris when I become all feathers I will
Be a winged thing returning to homelands

We Learn to Hold the Sky

In Teotihuacan I swallowed breath after breath
until my estomago could hold no more
expansive azul, no more cotton candy nebullus.

As I walked la calle de los muertos
I placed hands on ash stone, climbed
stairs with nails gripping gray
                                    gray
                                        gray.

On la pirámide del Sol I learned
to say Dios without meaning God
or the dry bible pages I swallowed
before learning the wicked ways of words.
I learned to say Dios in the way I palm
keys like worry stones,

screamed Dios to part the clouds.
The palabra that pries open my chest
and gives way to the once contained
waters of my antepasados.

In Teotihuacan I became
reborn tickling feet with stone
holding the weight of ancient sangre.

This blood is a fractal of each mother
                                   father
                                         mother
and their children, broken,
forced to be brave until
Dios stepped out crying no more
                                no more
                                  no more.

History is a Winged Thing

I've learned of flight from mouths

        Been plucked from the ground and dragged   into
the air

before I was ready   before I could be transformed.

        I learned to be a rich, writhing, gusano so they'd consume me,
bury me

in their stomachs.   Let my body break down

        into something more theirs than my own—   a body
spineless

        and comfortable with being swallowed whole.

        I found myself in the well of their bellies.   I
thrived

in the acid.   Let my tongue spin itself into thread.

        Made of my body a cocoon.   In the echo

of solitude I got lost   in dreams of flight where I became
empty

        not instrument-hollow   but more   like endless caverns of
echoes.

I proclaimed myself a monarch.   Tore my cage and emerged winged

            willing to be Monarch   of all the caught and
devoured.

V.

Aesop Remix for my Hija: The Porcupine and the Snakes

I've lost myself in wondering how many pricks we should stand
before we allow ourselves to be lost to our venom.
I think being good is full of contradictions.
I'm not much for this bullshit idea that *everyone bites the hand that feeds,*

or giving means we'll always be robbed. I think, Hija,
sometimes you gotta give more love than you should.
I think it's good to be a giver in this world cuz there's not much

being given. And truth is, we can poison-burn too.
Truth is, sometimes our rattles keep others up
all night. Sometimes we're so smooth and charming we don't realize
how tightly we're holding. And yeah, maybe there will be a point
when the prick will fuck up in some kind of way,

and maybe then it's time to reclaim your space,
but what I'm trying to say is that you don't stop giving just in case.
But if you're robbed or forced out of a home
that once felt safe it's alright to bite back. Only then though.
I don't know, maybe I'm setting you up to be too kind
to a world that doesn't deserve it. I'm just saying,

give people a chance, and if all that niceness shit fails,
look at your own blue veins. See, our blood holds all the DNA
of pricks that have come into our lives.
And maybe it's fine to let out a little poison from time to time.

An Ode to Nopales

My abuela picks off needles from nopales
one at a time, grasps them with tweezers and tugs
beneath the girasol in still water skies.

I could have been the one holding the machete
hacking away at nopales growing against
a chain link fence
while chickens wild around me.

Mama skillets onions to sun-kissed tan.
We cook for acceptance into a future
we've run from or run towards.
Bronze garlic and serrano peppers.
Toss in whisked eggs and chorizo.

When I prepare nopales I savor
their slime, their hint of lime
and barely-there sweetness
mix them with zanahorias, queso fresco,
and fresh plucked cilantro we grow in a can.

I walk alongside my hija eating salad,
swallowing whole slices and point out
the hills hold the secrets of pre-bordered history
when this land was ours and we its future.

I tell my hija coyotes have learned to survive famine
by eating freely dropped fruit
we have learned to be needle-topped
to survive. I tell her we must praise this land—
these families of nopales overcoming borders—
I tell her we must carry on in the words we speak
in the stories we thunder.

Hija, I Want You to Understand

I have praised this world through grinning
mentiras without mentioning how many times
I've wanted to shrink
and float through your fairy door, without
mentioning I am not as valorous
as this given name, see, I haven't been the most honest mother.

I have no excuses for you. I haven't prepared you
as a mother should. I know
I've stolen your fallen dientes only to hide
them among paperclips, pushpins, and
darkness, esas cosas you won't need
until you are old enough to know
there are no fairies to drag away these teeth.

And Hija, I never told you that survival
is living despite these realities.

One day I will explain,
lying always involves creating
some broken version of truth
and even diamonds crack
under their own weight, but Hija
how could I steal possibility
from your hands?

Hija, when you lost your teeth,
I gathered all of those loose and tumbling pearls
to craft you a necklace of your inocencia,
to thread them on your first strand of gray hair.
Even without this wisdom in your mouth
maybe you'll remember that I only ever taught you
to take a magnifying glass to the girasol
to find the world hidden in seeds—
even if weeds rise around you.

Las Mujeres Caídas

Call me an escultora. Watch me carve a spiral
staircase from pearl espina. Give you steps to claw and
leap from. You beg me, *Melt your teeth and make me
feathers. We'll learn of flight from hunger: mouths
hollowed by clouds.* I say I'm missing alas,
say I once swallowed crushed palomas, still the
fluttering lives inside my cage garganta. See me
wearing away their wings, each word unspoken
stealing their flight. I stare at mirrors, pray and
oracle futures while you say, *We own the power to
bake the estrellas, frost them with our lenguas.*
How can I explain Dios once gave me wings but
I chose to cloak myself instead, to watch
estrellas dance across the onyx skies.

In a Dream My Dead Tío Tells Me He's Happy

We're driving along looking for an all night bar
and I remember no one else but him, and how we laughed
how he stuck his head out the window
and howled. And in the dream neither one of us
talked about our love/hate relationship with tequila
or how we both had a tendency to sprout fangs
at a single mirada. Didn't matter if the eyes were
admiring or jealous. When we found the bar
we walked inside and I said, *wait,*
I have people I want you to meet! I said
they gotta see you now, like this. And my Tío said
he just wanted it to be him and I for a while, like this,
where his voice wasn't crackled by static
and a phone line, where I could see his face lit by neon
where his eyes weren't crazed weren't blocked
by metal bars, but smooth marbles with mountains
and forests inside, and all that damn glimmering brown.
So we smoked some mota and chilled. We talked shit
about the DJ and said, *this music's too mellow.*
Neither one of us wanted to move around anyways.
But the red warm of the room was making me think
about things like love and holding hands and I told my Tío
I had a man he needed to meet. But all he said was *Mija, you go.*

I gotta stay here a while longer. But te amo, he said as I left,
leaving him behind on a red velvet couch, chillin with a joint,
and clouds pillowing his head.

La Caída

I can never find the línea
of the horizon over the waves that puff
into algodon clouds. I swear
I see silence in the tumble
of foam, but my hands
only make it dissolve, and I hate
that my intent is to capture
todo en mis manos.
When we fuck there is no crash
we move until solo sal is in our teeth
and my tongue is the color of drought.
I am silenced by the polished-glass clinking
outside our beach-cottage bodies and the chime
of our vibrating laughs. The ocean never threatens
to run out of noise and sky. The waves
will never agree to forgo their whip
for our voices. And I, I never noticed
your eyes are a conch shell I lean to
listening for an echo of some contained
version of myself. But I glimpse the infinity
in the solitary grain and,
Dios, I praise this sea, this endless sea. I beg
just give us more time and I'll weave
these prayers into the feathers of the flying fish.

Mudskippers[4]

We survive outside our homes of water.
Learn to breathe from the air that lives within our mouths.
We look over the mess that surrounds us
seek out all the splashing brown, the happy brown,
the vividly living or just surviving brown.
In this muck we know we are not welcome:
we are strange and clumsy to the landwalkers.
Us with our ojos living above our heads
to see every which way because we have been plucked
here or forced to run here. We know so little
of the predators other than they do not like
our ability to survive in the between.
So we push through the heavy.
Home becomes the space we move through.
And we move tirelessly. We carry the water from our casitas
in our cheeks and savor the freshness savor how it felt to breathe
surrounded with beings like us. We exist by rationing the water,
knowing there's a chance we might never get to swim again.

---

[4] Mudskippers are known for being a fish with the interesting ability to survive both in and out of water.

A Sonnet of Pasos

My hija dances more than she walks. Quilts together
mastered steps: feet floating like the wind under feathers
or turning petals bracing for a fall that never
tumbles. My Hija dances: mariposa wings untethered.

I whisper lullabies about the moon's song and the way it bleeds
from her feet but my Hija peers beyond glistening eyes, sees
tunes caught between the caged bird's beak
and she, with her glimmering existence, tugs them unleashed.

My Hija embraces the world where love is the only poder
that matters. When she asks why I cry when she dances
I say, "Tu Corazón canta de un mundo que deseo conocer."
A world that has never beat her. Where chances

are decided by precisely tuned steps strung
together; a rhythm that has yet to be sung.

Umbilical

Sangre only rusts because of oxygen
and maybe, Hija, I'm not full of all the magia

I'd like you to believe. Maybe it's all science
and maybe everything I pass on
can be explained by a research paper or years of experiments.

I believe truth exists in the paradox
like how sueños are more like fog:
suspended time
where even the water is willing
to be still.

It's funny how we only ever see one side of La Luna.
All this time we look up and we think we know her.

Maybe you and I are like that.
Maybe we're made to orbit the galaxy all the way

to Pluto's sunken corzón only ever showing one side.

But imagine all our shadow sees,
all that endless night.

When you wake, I still have to shake
comets from your lashes and some nights
I hear the rings of Saturn in your breath.

Sometimes you leave the place you were born for,
and maybe you come back new, feeling unseen.
Every scratched knee is a reminder you were willing to risk
it all to fly for a moment. Every broken heart
recorded in photos turned ash is a reminder
you are more than the dust you leave behind.

I'm trying to understand how to be human,
and trying to show you what it means.

In Gratitude

There's something that happens when we reach this part of the making of the book, a kind of overwhelm of gratitude for all who are involved in the making of it, both physically and spiritually. Forgive me if you're important to me and your name has somehow slipped my mind. There are so many names, so many spirits, who I extend gratitude to.

I want to begin by thanking you, reader, for taking the time to tune into this little slice of my being. For being willing to sit with all of this and see the ways this writing might spark something new in you.

I want to extend a deep gratitude to my child. They have formed me into a new person by teaching me about autonomy, identity, teaching me to see the truth behind didactic stories and lessons. More than anything, I want to thank them for opening my sight to a new version of myself. I am excited to discover who you become, little one.

I'd like to take a moment to thank my partner, Tex, who has always praised my writing, believed in not just these words, but any seed of a dream I tried to hide from. I want to thank him for teaching me about embracing who I am and about being confident in finding the audience for my work. I'm eager to discover all we continue to create together.

Deepest gratitude to my family, both living and in the beyond. To my mother, I want you to know that I never felt like any dream was impossible. You taught me that happiness mattered most and whatever I desired was within reach, a truth that many don't often hear from parents. I thank my sister, who taught me about connection, about relating, about learning to see myself in others and them in me. My grandmother, who taught me to believe in more than what was physically in front of me, who taught me the value of life-skills and how to give love in the way we feed others, the way we tend to them. And gratitude to the spirits of my lineage who whisper poems and myths to me in sleep. Even the restless and frustrated spirits because without them I would have never pushed myself and my family towards growth.

I want to take a moment to thank everyone at Sundress who was involved in the making of this book, everyone who believed in the words and who saw what it could become even before I did.

In the same vein, I am grateful to my mentors: Blas Falconer who taught me to weave stories and a narrative in even the most abstract of my pieces. Ilya Kaminsky, who showed me the value in moving across borders, time, and space, to read poetry feverishly and to see even a seed of beauty in everything I read. Sandra Alcosser, who witnessed the shaping of this book from start to finish, and who pushed me to dig into the why of this manuscript. To Stephen Paul-Martin who believed in my weird little hybrid stories, who saw the image and understood all the lines of myths woven in them.

Gratitude to the members of my Tin House Cohort and Danez Smith, the guide of our lil group. Y'all showed me how to find community in my writing journey, you were willing to receive my works and see the beauty in them.

Finally, at least for this portion, I want to extend gratitude to readers of this work in its various stages who also became friends. Matt Fowler, a fellow

Cancerian, who unknowingly allowed me to find a space where I could be all of me, both on the page and outside of it. Tamaria del Rio, who's guidance in small changes showed me the importance of every word, every pause, every mark. Brandon Boynton, who's love of storytelling reminded me to consider the larger role each poem contributed to the whole of the book. Celeste Morales who created a space where I felt comfortable being both parent and creator, which is surprisingly difficult as a young mother.

While not a traditional note of thanks, I'm grateful to all of the spirits in my lives, the planets, the stars, the celestial beings, every essence that adds meaning and purpose to my day.

About the Author

V. Ruiz is a Queer Xicana astrologer, artist, and writer fascinated by language and the magic it evokes. They currently live in Los Angeles with their little one, underworld roaming pets, and partner. Aside from studying the cosmos, they also enjoy their work as an Associate Publisher for Row House Publishing. *In Stories We Thunder* is their debut collection. You can find them ranting about astrology and magic online as The Celestial Bruja.

Other Sundress Titles

the Colored page
Matthew E. Henry
$12.99

Slack Tongue City
Mackenzie Berry
$12.99

Year of the Unicorn Kidz
jason b. crawford
$12.99

Mouths of Garden
Barbara Fant
$12.99

Sweetbitter
Stacey Balkun
$12.99

Something Dark to Shine In
Inès Pujos
$12.99

Cosmobiological
Jilly Dreadful
$16.99

Slaughter the One Bird
Kimberly Ann Priest
$12.99

Dad Jokes From Late in the Patriarchy
Amorak Huey
$12.99

The Valley
Esteban Rodriguez
$12.99

What Nothing
Anna Meister
$12.99

To Everything There Is
Donna Vorreyer
$12.99

Hood Criatura
féi hernandez
$12.99

I Am Here to Make Friends
Robert Long Foreman
$14.99

nightsong
Ever Jones
$12.99

Maps of Injury
Chera Hammons
$12.99

JAW
Albert Abonado
$9.99

Lessons in Breathing Underwater
HK Hummel
$12.99

www.ingramcontent.com/pod-product-compliance
Lightning Source LLC
Chambersburg PA
CBHW081235090426
42738CB00016B/3309